CHECKRIDES

(Previously published as FLIGHT TESTS)

Jim Davis

First Edition published December 1981

Second Edition published July 2008

Third Edition published August 2022

This Edition published March 2026

By Jim's Famous Live Cowards' Club

CONTENTS

LIVING WITH FLIGHT TESTS

It's no use bleating. They — whoever they are — are trying to make sure you are a safe pilot. Flight Tests or Reviews are part of every pilot's life, so live with them.

Before setting sail, let's clear up a couple of things. We are not going to do the he/she his/her thing. In this book you will be tested by a girl called she, and you are a person called you. OK?

Also, we are not going to get excited about the difference between a test and a review. They are the same animal — only you can't fail a review, but you can be declared 'not yet competent,' for heaven's sake. It still means you have failed.

Finally, we are not going to delve into various countries' flight test procedures. If your stick and rudder work is OK, this little book will guide you easily through the practical flight test. It works beautifully for the American FAA, the

EASA (previously called European CAA), the South African CAA, and Australia's CASA.

If your handling skills are not good, I can't help you, and you are probably not a safe pilot. Get a good instructor and sort it out.

Most test failures are not caused by iffy handling. They are the result of poor checks, procedures, and airmanship.

That's what this little book is for. It takes you through each flying exercise and tells you what she expects of you. If you do what it says, you will pass easily and be a safer pilot — and we'll all be happy.

SERIOUS STUFF

OK, we are not going to take off. Taxi back and get your instructor to phone me. You have failed.

This happens — and rightly so. If you can't hack it on the ground, it's a waste of time getting into the air. It doesn't matter how good your steep turns are or how well you judge your forced landings, you will fail if your checks, procedures, and airmanship are not up to scratch — and she will find this out on the ground.

To pass you must have reasonable stick and rudder skills, but she also wants to see:

- You know your aircraft (what each antenna is for; max and min oil levels, etc.).
- Airmanship.
- Command ability.
- Common sense.
- Showmanship (yup, that's right — showmanship).

Don't panic, it's easy. Here are a couple of examples:

When you look out before starting the engine, don't glance — look. Look all round. Ask the examiner to look on her side. Open the storm window and shout 'Clear Prop!'

You get 100% for that. You have done the airmanship bit by making sure the prop is clear. You have demonstrated command ability by telling the other crew member what to do. It is common sense to use them to clear the blind spot. And the showmanship shows her that you are in command and doing the job properly.

Here's another example. Your landing checks should go like this:

Brakes — we have pressure in the toe-brakes and the park-brake is off.

Gear is fixed.

Mixture is fully rich.

Pitch is fixed.

Fuel is on the left main, the quantity is sufficient for a landing and go-around, the pressure is in the green and the pump is on.

Flaps — the speed is in the white and we select one notch.

You are not just mumbling your way through a checklist. You are doing the job properly and you are showing her that you are a professional.

Talking of checklists

For your pre-takeoff checks - use a good written list. For your checks in the air – you need to memorize mnemonics. You can't have your head in the cockpit while flying in a busy pattern. (Examples on pages 65 -- 67)

Under the heading of showmanship, tell her everything that's not obvious. When you do the engine run-up, tell her that the brakes are holding — otherwise how does she know that you would notice creep?

Every five minutes or so throughout the flight, tell her the temps and pressures are in the green — she has to know you are monitoring them. When you look for other traffic, really look and ask her to look on her side.

Don't be intimidated — treat her as an interested passenger. Don't trust her to do up her seat belt or close the door properly — check.

When she asks you to do a stall or a steep turn, don't just do it. Tell her you will do it when you are ready. Remember, she is an interested passenger. Do your HASELL checks first, and tell her what you are doing. Point out your forced landing field, and be sure it's a good one — she may make you use it.

If she fiddles with radios or other controls, she is expecting you to demonstrate command ability. Tell her to keep her hands and feet off the controls. Show her you are in charge.

And for this test, be sure you dress neatly — no flip-flops and T-shirts. She will be dressed smartly so you had better toe the line!

- Know your aircraft.
- Use airmanship.
- Show command ability — be the boss.
- Use common sense.
- Remember she is an interested passenger — don't be intimidated.
- Use showmanship — show her that you know what you are doing.

MAKE IT EASY FOR YOURSELF

- Talk to her before the test and clear up any questions you may have.
- Make sure your aircraft is clean and tidy.

- Make sure you are neatly and comfortably dressed.
- Turn up early. Being late and rushing will get you off to a bad start.
- Be mentally prepared for the test — that's what this little book is for.
- Don't bring your business or domestic worries with you.
- Have a good breakfast. If you don't eat, your flying will suffer. Seriously, don't let pre-test nerves prevent you from eating.
- Think of the examiner as an interested passenger.
- Make sure that there are no misunderstandings in the cockpit.
- Don't be afraid to ask her exactly what she wants you to do.
- If you make a mistake, forget about it and concentrate on the next exercise.
- Plan ahead of the aircraft the whole time.
- From time to time, tell her that you are checking temps and pressures.
- Remember that good engine handling is the hallmark of a good pilot.

Try to do everything smoothly. Imagine that you have your 90-year-old granny in the back, and it's her first flight ever. Do everything smoothly — even small things like applying carb heat, changing power settings, or selecting flap. Passengers should not be able to notice changes of power, speed, and attitude.

Checks, procedures, and airmanship are the essence of this little book. If you have got most of it in your head, you can stop worrying and enjoy the flight.

PRE-TEST PREPARATION

Here's stuff to get your head around before she arrives. You must:

- Have the latest NOTAMs and have the FARs, the AIM, and relevant advisory circulars available — and know roughly where to find things.
- Understand weather reports, forecasts, and weather charts.
- Know what servicing operations you are allowed to carry out on the airplane.
- Know how to operate all the aircraft's systems — oxygen, autopilot, pressurization, de-icing, etc.
- Know how to deal with an engine fire during startup. Switch off the fuel and keep cranking the starter. If this fails, switch off the master and mags, get out, and direct the fire extinguisher onto the carburetor — usually at the bottom of the engine.
- Know how to deal with a cabin fire. Ventilate the cabin and try to put the fire out. If this fails, land smartly.
- Know how to handle an engine fire in flight. Ventilate the cabin, switch off the fuel, sideslip the flames to one side, and land ASAP.
- Know how to handle a static port blockage causing the ASI, VSI, and altimeter to go unserviceable. Use the alternate static source — see the POH.
- Know how to handle an alternator/generator failure. Conserve battery power. Possible radio failure — know non-radio procedures.
- Know how to operate the emergency gear extension and any other emergency procedure applicable to type — see the POH.

- Be able to work out weight and balance and performance on your aircraft — takeoff distance, climb, range, and so on with various loads and density altitudes.
- Know the privileges and limitations of the certificate you are going for.

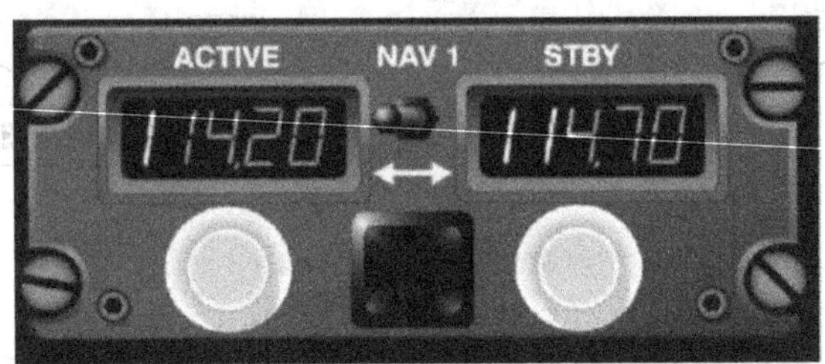

PREFLIGHT INSPECTION

She will form an impression of you in the first few minutes, so get off to a good start by doing a professional job of your preflight.

Before she arrives, make sure:

- The aircraft is clean and tidy — no soda cans under the seats.
- It's legally airworthy and carries all the correct paperwork.
- Everything works. Compass card, fire extinguisher, etc., are current.
- Luggage, equipment, fire axe, and so on are properly stowed.
- There is enough fuel and oil for the flight, plus reserves.
- The windshield and side windows are clean.
- The aircraft is parked intelligently.

She will want to see you do a preflight according to the POH. You must know the aircraft and be ready to answer questions on it. She might ask you what voltage the electrical system is, or ask you to explain a pipe under the fuselage (battery vent).

Tell her what you are doing if it isn't obvious. When you test the fuel, don't just glance at the sample and chuck it away. Tell her that it has no water or dirt, it's the right color, and it smells like fuel.

Brief her on emergency procedures, and the whereabouts and operation of the ELT, first-aid kit, and fire extinguisher.

Tell her to keep her hands and feet off the controls.

The preflight does not end when you get in the airplane. Continue checking everything inside the cockpit in a set order. Work out a round-the-cockpit sequence to use every time you fly — perhaps top-to-bottom, then left-to-right and right-to-left as in the diagram. It works well for most aircraft, but if you want to invent your own system that's fine — just make sure you use the same sequence every time.

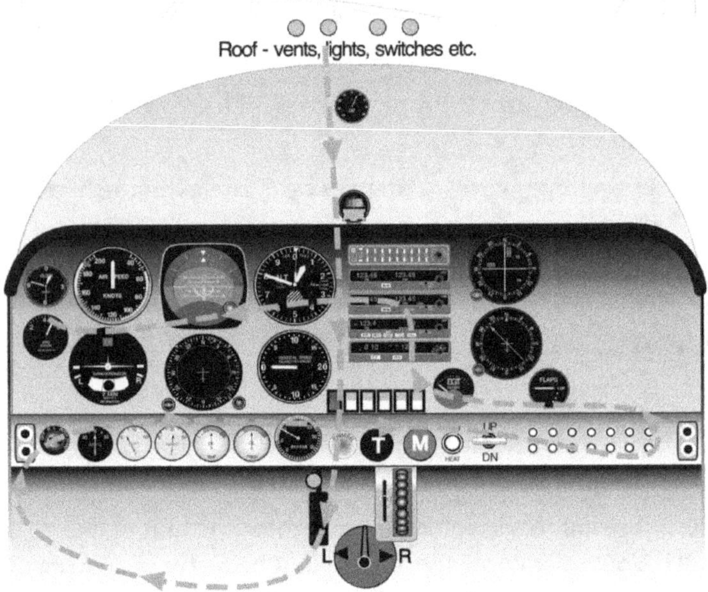

These checks should include (but are not limited to):

- Brakes set.
- Trimmers set to neutral.
- Flaps up.
- Fuel selected.
- Gear selected down.
- All electrics switched off.
- All radios off.
- All circuit breakers set.
- The instruments that should show zero do show zero.

- Other instruments OK (e.g., manifold pressure 30" minus 1" per 1,000' AMSL).
- The compass looks serviceable, the fluid is clear, and the card is current.
- The clock wound up and set to UTC.
- The altimeter is set to field elevation. Note the altimeter setting.

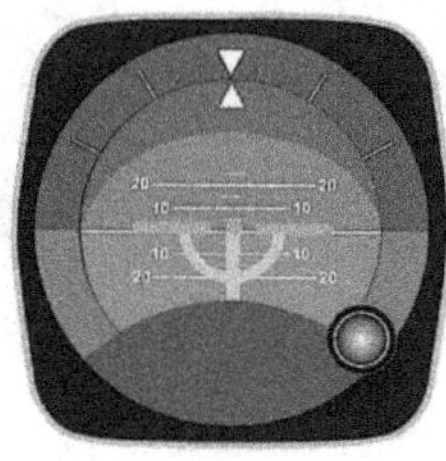

GROUND HANDLING

Checks Before Starting

When you have done your round-the-cockpit checks, you have finished the preflight.

Now use a written list if you like for the POH start procedure. Before you hit the starter, make sure the prop is clear and get her to check her side.

Checks After Starting

Check the oil pressure goes into the green within 30 seconds. (Put a finger on the gauge and keep it there while you watch the second hand of the clock.)

At the same time, adjust the throttle to 1,000 rpm. Nothing annoys her more than an engine that races to 1,500 rpm as soon as it starts.

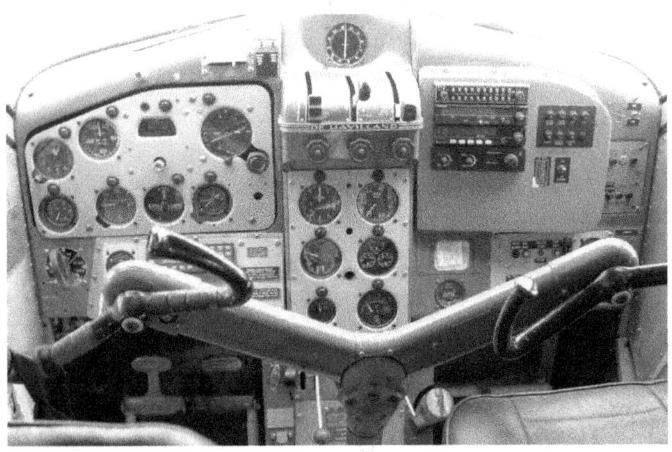

Now do your round-the-cockpit check again, paying special attention to:

- Engine instruments coming into the normal operating range.
- Fuel pump off (if applicable).
- Fuel pressure still in the green with the pump off.
- Anti-collision lights on.
- Other electrical switches as needed.
- Circuit breakers set.
- Alternator charging.
- Gyro suction 4–5".
- Radios on, frequencies and selector switches set.
- Navigation radios on.
- Beacons identified and correct indications checked.
- Heading Indicator set.
- Other gyros stabilized.
- All other instruments showing normal readings.

I throttle fully back now and do a mag dead-cut check, but not everyone agrees that this should be done.

Warm-Up

Know what the POH says. Some Continental engines like you to wait for the oil temperature to get into the green before takeoff, while Lycomings call for minimum ground running and want you to get into the air as soon as practical.

Radio

Your radio procedures are a huge giveaway. Mess up and she will view you sideways throughout the test. Remember to:

- Listen before transmitting.
- Prepare your message before hitting the PTT button.
- Have the mike very close to your mouth.
- Use a normal conversational voice at dictation speed.
- Use standard words and phrases.
- Anticipate the runway from the windsock and the altimeter setting from your altimeter.
- Use your call sign to show you received and understood the whole message.
- Ask ATC to 'Say again' if you don't understand any part of the message.
- Don't clutter the frequency with unnecessary chatter.
- For VFR flights, read back clearances, frequencies, and altimeter settings.
- Your initial call is to establish contact — e.g., "Podunk Ground, Cherokee Mike Victor on 121.9."
- When they reply, say: "Taxi for the training area. One plus one."
- When you get taxi clearance, read back: "Runway 08. 30.21. Cherokee Mike Victor."

Use of Engine and Brakes

This is tricky. It's stupid to use power against the brakes, but it's also bad to let the engine idle too slowly. This is a problem if you taxi downhill or downwind on a smooth surface. As brake linings are cheaper than engines, it's normally best to maintain about 1,000 rpm and use brakes to keep the speed in check. If you have to do this, tell her so she knows that you know.

To start taxiing, first throttle fully back, then release the brakes and use enough power to get moving. Throttle back again and bring it to a full stop to test the brakes.

When you are on the ramp or amongst other aircraft, keep your speed down to a fast walking pace. In the open you can go a bit faster. But you are more likely to lose points for taxiing too fast than for going too slowly.

Keep one hand on the throttle or brake at all times.

Maneuvering

For direction, use the rudder and a bit of toe or heel brake if necessary for sharper turns. If you have direct rudder-to-nosewheel steering (like the older Cherokees), do not use brake to turn — it scuffs the nosewheel sideways over the ground. If your steering is through springs, it's OK to use brake to tighten a turn, but only after you have full rudder.

Keep the nosewheel on the centerline and only move to the right when passing another aircraft. At the holding point, stop so you have a good view of base and finals. In a strong wind you may need to turn into wind for engine cooling.

If you have to backtrack, stop facing off the runway and into the pattern. This gives you a decent view of base and finals and allows you to pull off the runway if you need to get out of the way of a landing aircraft. Once you have stopped, put on the park-brake firmly for the run-up.

RUN-UP AND VITAL ACTIONS

Run-Up

The run-up is not just for a mag check. It's to let you check the overall health of the engine and propeller under power.

Smoothly increase to 1,800 rpm (or whatever the POH specifies) and glance out to make sure you are not creeping forward against the brakes. (Tell her the brakes are holding.) Set the revs exactly.

Check the following instruments are indicating correctly: oil pressure, oil temperature, EGT, vacuum, and manifold pressure.

Smoothly lean the mixture and mention the slight increase in rpm and EGT. When she starts getting rough — no, the engine, not she — return to fully rich.

Check the carb heat if you are not on a dusty surface. Check the operation of the pitch control — once only. I have no idea where this 'three times' business comes from. It's not in any POH I have ever seen.

Check each mag. Say what the drops are and tell her the maximum permissible and the maximum difference between drops.

Throttle smoothly right back to check the slow idle and to confirm the engine doesn't die when the throttle is closed (which could be caused by carb icing).

Return to 1,000 rpm.

Now, after you have confirmed everything is normal with the engine and its controls, you can do the vital actions.

Vital Actions

If you have a good written list, use it. If you have a list in your head, that's also fine. Do it slowly and methodically and say what you are doing. Touch each instrument or control as you check it. Muttering 'Mixture rich, mags on both...' is not good enough. Say clearly, 'The mixture is fully rich,' and at the same time feel the mixture control to make sure it's right forward. When you say 'Mags on both,' feel the switches to make sure they are both on. Do all the checks like this. Don't assume she has closed her door properly or secured her seat belt firmly. It is up to you to check these things.

Here's a tried-and-trusted checklist that covers all the important items on most light aircraft. If you don't have a good list, I suggest you use this one. Either stick the initials on the panel or read it off a written list. (Examples on pages 65 -- 67)

AIRMANSHIP

This means using common sense, being wide awake to what's going on around you, and anticipating consequences. For instance, if you are going to cross another runway or taxiway, look and listen for traffic long before you get there, then call the tower and get permission to cross. Lower the sun visors before turning into the sun. Keep the wind direction in mind at all times. Think about the movement of other traffic in relation to what you are and will be doing.

Radio

Use the principles listed in the Ground Handling section. Also:

- Listen to other traffic — don't request takeoff with an aircraft on finals.
- Use the VOR test point if available.
- Listen to the ATIS and tell ATC that you have 'Information Delta' or whatever.
- If you have a No. 2 VHF or a standby frequency, tune it to the next station.

TAKEOFF

Safety Measures

When you have done your vital actions:

- Check on base and finals for other aircraft.
- Be aware of wake turbulence from recent traffic.
- Tell ATC that you are ready.
- Line up on the centerline using every inch of runway.
- Stop very briefly with the nosewheel or tailwheel straight.
- Check the windsock.
- Check for aircraft or vehicles using other runways.
- Check the compass and DI against the runway heading.
- Do not recheck your vital actions — you are blocking the runway.
- Make sure your feet are off the toe or heel brakes.

It shouldn't take more than five seconds to check the windsock, the compass and DI, and look for traffic on the other runways. If it does, everyone will get annoyed with you — including her!

Application of Power

Move the throttle smoothly and positively fully forward. This should also take about five seconds.

Keep your hand on the throttle and tell her the engine is delivering full power — for example, '2,350 rpm' or '28 inches and 2,700 rpm. Temps and pressures in the green.'

On turbocharged or supercharged engines, don't let the manifold pressure exceed the takeoff limit.

Heading During Run

- Use the rudder to keep straight on the centerline as you increase power.
- Anticipate weathercocking if there is a crosswind.
- Anticipate the gyroscopic swing as the tailwheel lifts (if applicable), or
- Anticipate the need for more rudder as the nosewheel lifts (tricycle types).

Handling the Control Column

How you do this depends on a whole bunch of things:

- The type of aircraft.
- The runway surface.
- The density altitude.
- The runway gradient.
- Obstacles to be cleared after takeoff.
- Wind conditions.
- Runway length.
- Load in the aircraft.

On some tailwheel types, it's best to let the tail fly up when it is ready. Others like you to raise the tail as soon as possible.

Many conventional aircraft like a slight back pressure to get the weight off the nosewheel. Others with laminar flow wings should accelerate in a level attitude.

On a rough or soft surface, you should get some of the weight off the wheels as soon as possible.

High-density altitudes call for acceleration with minimum aerodynamic drag — this means keeping the nose level. Same for short fields.

If the runway slopes, a nose-level attitude means level with the ground, not the horizon.

If it is a short field with obstacles to clear, do what the POH says. Also know what the POH says about soft-field techniques.

If it's gusty, add the strength of the gusts to your liftoff speed. So if it's gusting from 15 to 25 kts (i.e., 10-knot gusts) and you usually lift off at 60 kts, then your new liftoff speed will be 70 kts. Tell her you are going to do this because some sources call for adding half the gust.

So much for the elevator. If there's a crosswind you will also be using the ailerons. Hold the stick fully into wind initially. Then as the airspeed increases you will need less aileron to keep the wings level. (See Crosswind Takeoff & Landing.)

Handling After Leaving the Ground

Remember to:

- Keep the wings level as you leave the ground. Don't drop the right wing (clockwise prop).
- Level the nose to accelerate to best-rate-of-climb speed.
- Use enough rudder to counteract power.

Do the after-takeoff checks at 400' AGL or when there is no usable runway ahead. (Examples on pages 65 -- 67)

Climb Attitude, Airspeed, and Direction

The nose attitude will dictate your airspeed. Immediately after liftoff, level the nose and allow the aircraft to accelerate to its climb speed.

Then raise the nose to the climb attitude for that flap setting.

When you raise the flaps, change the attitude to maintain your climb speed.

You should nominate climb speed before takeoff. If you have to clear obstacles, use the best angle of climb speed from the POH. Otherwise use the best rate of climb speed. For a cross-country, use the cruise-climb figure.

Track along the runway's extended centerline, allowing for any crosswind. Do this by turning slightly into wind and crabbing — not by lowering a wing or getting the ball out of the middle!

Engine Failure During / After Takeoff

She may do this:

- When you are still on the ground.
- After you are airborne with usable runway ahead.

After you are airborne with **no** usable runway ahead.

If you are on the ground, throttle right back and use the brakes as needed.

If you are in the air and there is usable runway ahead, throttle right back, lower the nose into glide attitude, use full flaps, land, and brake as needed.

If there is no usable runway, 'Speed Field Fuel Flap' is a useful checklist. (Examples on pages 65 -- 67)

NEVER TURN BACK TO THE FIELD!

CLIMBING TURNS

Safety Measures

You should be at least 500' AGL when you start a climbing turn. Have a good look around for other traffic before entering and during the turn. On slower aircraft, increase your airspeed by 5 to 10 kts.

Going In

Roll in smoothly, using enough rudder to counteract aileron drag and power.

Accuracy of Turn

Keep a steady 20° or 25° of bank throughout the turn. Use rudder to keep the ball in the middle. Due to the effects of power, you will probably have to use right rudder even in a left turn.

Control of Attitude, Speed, and Direction

Allow for the attitude looking different during right and left turns. Keep to your nominated airspeed (plus the 5 to 10 kts on slower types).

She will tell you to turn toward a specific point or onto a particular heading. Be sure you understand her properly, and then do what she wants.

In the pattern, use visual references to make sure you roll out exactly square, or parallel, to the runway. If there's a wind, allow for it and tell her you are doing so.

Coming Out

Maintaining your lookout, roll smoothly out of the turn using enough rudder to counteract aileron drag and power. On slower types, raise the nose slightly to return to normal climb speed.

MEDIUM TURNS

Have a good lookout and then roll in smoothly, using enough rudder to counteract aileron drag.

Maintain 30° of bank and keep the ball in the middle. On most aircraft the ball will stay there on its own once you are settled in the turn and the ailerons are neutral.

In a medium turn, control your airspeed and altitude with the elevator. Keep a slight back pressure to maintain the correct attitude, and the altitude will stay constant. The airspeed will decrease slightly.

Maintain a good lookout throughout the turn.

Roll out smoothly to the predetermined heading, again using enough rudder to counteract aileron drag.

STEEP TURNS

Safety Measures

Treat a steep turn as an aerobatic maneuver — it might become one if you mess it up. So you need to do HASELL checks first.

Going Into the Turn

As you roll through 30° of bank, smoothly increase power, using enough rudder to counteract power and aileron drag. Stop the roll at 45° or 60° (as briefed).

Accuracy of Turn

Maintain the 45° or 60° of bank using the horizon and/or the attitude indicator. Keep the ball in the middle with the rudder. (Once you are established in the turn, you will only need a little rudder to counteract the extra power.)

Airspeed and Altitude

Once the turn is stable, there is nothing you can do about the airspeed. It will settle at a figure determined by the power and bank angle. Use the elevator to maintain altitude and the airspeed will look after itself.

The story about using top rudder to keep the nose up is nonsense. Don't do it.

Coming Out

Smoothly reduce to cruise power as the bank goes through 30°. As you roll out, use enough rudder to counteract aileron drag and the power reduction.

STEEP GLIDING TURNS AND SPIRAL DIVES

She can ask you to do a steep (40°-banked) gliding turn. Do your HASELL checks first. As you go through 30°, increase your airspeed by 10–15 kts.

She may ask you to let it develop into a spiral dive and then recover by leveling the wings and pulling out of the dive.

STALLS

For a normal stall, when she tells you to do a stall, she doesn't mean right this second. She means when you are ready.

She wants to see if you know exactly when the aircraft stalls, so say 'there she goes' when the wings let go — not at the onset of the buffet.

Do your HASELL checks: (Examples on pages 65 -- 67)

I will talk you through a clean stall with no power. She may want you to use other configurations, but the principle is the same.

She will want to see that you:

- Close the throttle fully and smoothly.
- Use sufficient rudder to counteract loss of power and decreasing airspeed.
- Ease the nose slightly up and continue easing back to maintain altitude.
- Keep in balance with the rudder.
- Keep the wings level with coordinated aileron and rudder.
- Maintain a constant altitude by steadily easing the nose up with the elevator.

She may want you to stall with the gear up or down, the flaps at different settings, and different power settings. Tell her that the airspeed is within limits when you select gear or flap. Make sure you correct any pitch changes smoothly and positively. Remember to set cowl flaps, carb heat, and pitch as required. Do the HASELL checks before each stall. Don't wander out of the training area during the exercise.

Symptoms of the Stall

Mention the following symptoms as they happen during each stall:

- Decreasing airspeed.
- Sloppy controls.
- Stall warning.
- Pre-stall buffet.

Method of Recovery

She will tell you which sort of recovery to use:

- With power — to climb.
- With power — to straight and level with minimum altitude loss.
- Without power — to a glide.

She will be watching that you:

- Ease the stick smoothly forward (to break the stall).
- At the same time, smoothly apply full power.
- Use sufficient rudder to counteract the yaw caused by the power.
- Go to climb attitude as soon as you have climb speed.
- Keep the wings level throughout.
- Use the engine controls and cowl flaps sensibly.

To recover with minimum altitude loss, ease the nose into the level attitude as soon as possible without inducing a secondary stall. At cruise speed, reduce to cruise power.

To recover to a glide, ease the stick forward to break the stall, and adopt the glide attitude. Adjust engine controls, cowl flaps, and trim as required.

During recovery you will lose points if you bang the stick forward and induce negative G. Ditto if you don't get it forward enough and induce a secondary stall, or if you recover from the nose-down attitude too sharply and cause a secondary stall. You have to get it just right.

Use of the Engine

She will be watching your engine handling throughout. Remember to:

- Set the cowl flaps as required.
- Set the mixture fully rich.
- Set the pitch fully fine.
- Put the carb heat on (depending on type).
- Throttle back smoothly and fully.
- Smoothly apply full power for recovery, and
- After recovery, set the power to climb or cruise settings as required.

SPINS AND INCIPIENT SPINS

RELAX. This is only for instructors, phew!

If the aircraft is certified for spins, she will want you to do them. If it's not, then you must recover at the incipient stage — as soon as you see it's about to spin.

Do the HASELL checks: (Examples on pages 65 -- 67)

To initiate a spin, the aircraft must stall positively and the stick must be held fully back until you want to recover.

To enter a spin, you need to get one wing stalled and not the other. You can do it with or without power, with crossed controls, or with the ailerons neutral.

In the test, the most usual entry is from a power-off stall using full rudder as she stalls. But this is not a realistic version of what is likely to happen accidentally in real life.

An accidental spin is most likely to happen when you try to clear an obstacle in a climbing turn (known as a departure stall), or when you try to stretch a glide while turning finals. In either case the spin may be into or out of the turn.

Discuss this with her before the flight so there is no doubt about what she wants.

Whatever the method, use firm, positive pro-spin controls and maintain them on the stops until you want to recover. Then again be firm and positive. With many aircraft, the rate of rotation increases dramatically if you let the stick move forward even slightly. Close the throttle fully as the spin starts.

Method of Recovery

Normally incipient spin recovery is identical to that for a full spin:

- Throttle fully back.

- Use full anti-spin rudder.
- Pause.
- Move the stick smoothly forward until rotation stops.
- Level the wings.
- Ease smoothly and firmly out of the dive.

Return to level flight or a climb as directed. Adjust the power and cowl flaps as needed. Do not use power during the nose-down or high-speed portions of the recovery.

Use of Engine

Before you enter the spin or incipient, make sure the cowl flaps are closed, the mixture is rich, the pitch is fine, the carb heat is set as required. Handle the throttle smoothly and firmly.

When you have recovered, make sure the carb heat is off, then smoothly apply power. Set the rpm, mixture, and cowl flaps as necessary.

ASYMMETRIC FLIGHT

If you get an engine failure on the ground — throttle back immediately and stop.

In the air, correctly identifying the failed engine is a pass/fail aspect of the test and a live/die aspect of real life. I suggest you use the dead-foot, dead-engine method. Then confirm it by smoothly throttling back the suspect engine.

Don't rush the identification. When the engine fails:

- Fly the aircraft — maintain heading and at least blue-line speed.
- Use full power — unless it's not necessary.
- Retract the gear and flap intelligently (or according to the POH).
- After identifying, check for obvious causes — fuel, mag switches, etc.
- Confirm the identification with the throttle.
- Feather (if the examiner wants it) and clean up.

If the airspeed approaches VMC, you must either lower the nose or reduce power on the good engine.

You must use the rudder immediately to maintain directional control. Subsequently also use rudder trim and up to 5° of bank into the good engine. (Imagine riding on the live engine, or think of 'raising the dead.')

Anticipate and correct yaw during feathering and unfeathering of the prop.

Serious loss of directional control is a pass/fail, live/die issue.

She will mark you on initial and subsequent control of direction and altitude.

She may ask you to maintain blue-line, climb, or descend at a particular rate.

She may also ask you to maintain a particular airspeed.

Anticipate and correct airspeed and yaw changes during cleanup, as well as during feathering and unfeathering.

I recommend reciting the following self-briefing before takeoff in any multi-engine aircraft:

- If I have a directional problem I will abort immediately.
- I will rotate at 71 kts (red line + 5). I'll retract the gear when I have positive climb and accelerate to 89 kts (blue line).
- If I have an engine failure below 76 kts (best angle of climb) I will be prepared to throttle fully back and land.
- If I have an engine failure above 76 kts, I will: Fly the aircraft — maintain direction with rudder, and at least 76 kts. Power up — all levers fully forward. Gear up. Flaps up. Identify — dead foot, dead engine. Confirm — throttle back suspect engine. Think. Feather. Bank up to 5° towards the good engine. Plan — (e.g., left hand on to runway 05).

Touch each control as you say it — muscle memory works very well.

Cleaning Up

Once everything is under control, you need to:

- Make sure the gear is fully retracted and hasn't sagged slightly.
- Confirm the flaps are fully retracted.
- Close the cowl flaps on the feathered engine.
- Make sure the canopy, windows, and other drag items are closed.
- Check rudder and elevator trims.

- Use up to 5° of bank towards the good engine for minimum drag.
- Fully retard the throttle, mixture, and pitch controls on the dead engine.
- Switch off the mags on the dead engine.
- Switch off the alternator on the dead engine.
- Set exact power and mixture requirements on the good engine.
- Set the cowl flaps as required on the good engine.
- Check the fuel situation and cross-feed if necessary.
- Check the vacuum supply from the good engine.
- If an alternator dies with the engine, switch off equipment to conserve the battery.
- Make sure you have hydraulic power for the gear and flaps (if applicable).
- Plan gear and flap operation if electric or hydraulic power is not available.
- Replan your flight to divert or continue with revised ETAs and altitudes.
- Inform ATC.
- Monitor temps and pressures on the good engine.

You will never remember all this, so use your round-the-cockpit check sequence.

Asymmetric Maneuvering

She may ask you to maneuver the aircraft at various speeds down to VMC. You will be marked on smoothness, coordination, and awareness of the problems associated with asymmetric flight.

She may give you turns into and away from the dead engine as well as climbs and descents. Keep your handling gentle and maintain the airspeed above VMC.

She may also ask you to fly in various configurations of gear, flaps, and ancillaries. Make sure you are familiar with the aircraft's handling and that you know the systems and important items from the POH.

If she wants you to do a single-engine landing, the whole thing hinges on intelligent planning of the pattern. Maintain plenty of altitude and use gentle turns.

Only lower the gear and flaps when you can easily make the field with minimal power. If you have lost the power source for gear and flaps, make sure that you have enough time to operate the emergency systems.

It's potentially dangerous to attempt an asymmetric go-around in the landing configuration at low altitude — but it can be included in the test, for heaven's sake!

Unfeathering Procedures

Go through your normal pre-start procedures before unfeathering. Anticipate and correct the yaw caused by unfeathering. Give the engine time to warm up before using power. Anticipate and correct yaw during power changes as you start using the unfeathered engine.

Remember to reset all the systems and ancillary equipment to their normal operating positions. You may need to cross-feed to balance the fuel load. Again, use your round-the-cockpit check so you don't forget anything.

She will be looking at your general smoothness, coordination, planning, decision making, knowledge of the systems, handling of ancillaries, engine management, judgment, and your control of airspeed, attitude, and direction throughout.

FORCED LANDING

This can happen at any time during the test, so keep a good lookout for decent fields and keep the wind direction in your head.

Actually, most examiners give you an engine failure soon after you have done your HASELL checks. So pick a good field.

When the engine stops, use the excess airspeed to get you around the turn towards the field. If the field happens to be straight ahead, hold the nose level until you reach glide speed. Converting speed to altitude doesn't work on light aircraft.

Field Selection

When you select your field, think about the following:

- It must be within easy gliding distance.
- The surface wind speed and direction.
- The position of the sun — particularly if it is early morning or late evening.
- The slope of the field.

- Obstacles on the approach and overshoot ends.
- Its proximity to habitation.
- The possibility of wires, particularly near roads.

Cockpit Procedures

When the engine fails, do the following three things simultaneously:

- Close the throttle.
- Change tanks.
- Do a gliding turn towards the field.

Plan your descent, then do the following:

ENGINE: Check for the cause of the problem. Then smoothly go to full power and back to idle. With a simulated engine failure, this serves as a warm-up. With a real one, it is a test to see if you cured the problem by changing tanks and so on. In a real situation (and advise your examiner of this), you would shut down the engine if you can't restart it. Switch off fuel, close the throttle, mixture to idle-cutoff, mags off, and all unnecessary electrics off. Leave the master switch on until final approach.

MAYDAY: Make your Mayday call, or simply tell ATC what's happening if you are not in 'grave and imminent danger and in need of immediate assistance.'

PAX: Remind her of your emergency briefing. Tell her what's going on and make sure her seat belt is tight. Ask her to remove false teeth, glasses, and sharp objects from her pockets. Tell her how to brace herself. Remind her where the fire extinguisher, first-aid kit, and ELT are. Tell her how to unlatch the door, and explain any other emergency procedures.

BUMPFF: Carry out your normal landing checks. But don't select gear and flaps until you need them to steepen your approach. It's generally best to land with the gear down regardless of the terrain — it absorbs initial deceleration and keeps the fuel tanks off the ground. With high-wing aircraft, it may be better to keep the gear up if the surface is soft. Do whatever the POH and common sense call for.

Don't forget to do engine warm-ups at least every 1,000', or more frequently if your engine needs it.

Plan of Descent

There are several ways of planning your descent. They are all designed to get you to about 1,000' on base — a familiar position from which you would normally start a glide approach.

Keep the following in mind:

- Don't turn your back on the field.
- Keep the field in sight — don't have your head in the cockpit too long.
- Use ground features as a guide to your base-leg position.
- Don't rely on the altimeter. You won't know the altimeter setting or the height of the ground.
- Don't get too far from the field.
- Don't get so close you are forced to do steep turns. This is a common fault.
- Don't change your mind about field selection without a very good reason.
- Don't use gear or flaps until you are on your last base or final approach.
- If you have to steepen a gliding turn, use more airspeed.

Final Line

When you turn from base to finals, you should be a bit high. If you undershoot, you fail — and die! In real life you can stretch the glide quite a lot by pulling the propeller into fully coarse pitch. Don't do this in the test or when practicing — it takes so long to return to fine pitch again that you can't go around.

When you are high on finals, you can use the gear, flaps, and sideslipping to adjust the approach. Remember that the Cessna 100 and 200 series aircraft don't allow sideslipping with full flap.

Procedure on Final Approach

To steepen the approach, use the gear first, then the various stages of flap and sideslipping if the POH permits it with flap. In the test, the wings must be level by 400' AGL. On finals, mention that the fuel, mags, and master would go off — after you have used the electric power to lower the gear and flaps, if applicable. Also say that you would ask her to unlatch the door and jam it open with her shoe.

If you are not landing on an airfield, she will give you an altitude at which to go around, or she will tell you when to do it. Be sure that you understand this instruction and follow it implicitly.

For the go-around, put the carb heat off and smoothly apply full power. Now retract the gear and the flaps in stages at a safe airspeed and altitude.

Climb away at the best rate of climb speed, or the best angle of climb speed if you need to clear obstacles. Then do your normal after-takeoff checks.

Radio Procedures

Use common sense. If you have told ATC of your movements and then find them interrupted by the test forced landing, you should tell them you are doing a simulated forced landing in a specified area. Emphasize the word 'simulated' so as not to panic them.

Tell her when you would make a Mayday call. She will probably test your Mayday procedures on the ground.

Tell ATC your intentions after completing the test forced landing, and tell the examiner that in a real forced landing you would phone the tower when you are on the ground.

BAD WEATHER PATTERN AND PRECAUTIONARY LANDING

She will be watching your low flying. When she tells you to start looking for a field use one notch of flap and the best rate of climb speed. Select the best tank and switch on the pump. Trim slightly nose up, keep your hand on the throttle, and tell her you are aware of the wind and are looking out for birds, power lines, etc. (Actually the poles — because the lines are difficult to see.)

Use full flap for the approach. But if you are not actually landing and your aircraft climbs poorly with full flap, then use a smaller setting for the approach. Set the pitch and mixture so that you have full power when you need it. Check for carb icing frequently.

It is important to assess the wind early to help you choose a field. Keep the wind in mind during your patterns and correct for drift as necessary.

Inspection of Landing Path

Do a minimum of two inspection runs — one high and one at low level. The high-level one should be done at whatever altitude you are flying — generally 100' below the cloud base nominated by the examiner.

During the high-level inspection, check for:

- The general suitability of the field.
- The usable length.
- Obstructions on the approach and overshoot ends.
- The gradient.
- Its rough orientation on the compass or DI and relative to landmarks.
- Dams, roads, power lines, trees, etc.

- Animals — cattle, sheep, game.

If it looks generally suitable and safe, do a low-level inspection.

Fly just to the right of the landing path at about 50' and check the surface for mud, sand, long grass, ruts, holes, stones, and so on.

Make sure the airspeed doesn't increase during your descent for the low-level inspection. This is a common fault — you can't inspect it properly at high speed. Also don't let the airspeed bleed off during the inspection.

Remember:

- Do not get too far from the field — you may lose it in the poor visibility.
- Do not get so close that you have to do steep turns.
- Use left-hand patterns if possible, to keep the field on your side.
- Do not fly too close to the cloud base — it seriously reduces visibility.
- Use your DI and landmarks to help with orientation.

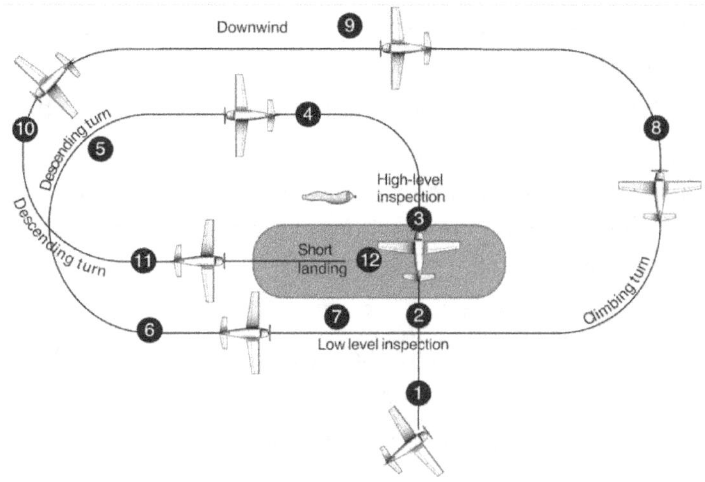

1. You see a suitable field and turn to fly over it. Select takeoff flap & best climb speed.
2. Look at general layout and prominent features.
3. High level inspection for orientation, approaches and general suitability.
4. Prepare for low level inspection. Best tank, pump on, mixture rich, pitch fine.
5. Descending turn.
6. Note direction and reciprocal on DG. Prepare to time the run.
7. Low level inspection of surface.
8. Climbing turn on to reciprocal.
9. Landing checks - BUMPFF.
10. Descending turn on to finals.
11. Select flap and airspeed for short landing.
12. After touchdown raise flap & brake firmly. Walk before taxiing. Phone ATC to cancel SAR.

Precautionary Pattern

1. You see a field that looks like it might be usable. Turn to fly straight over it. Select partial flap and use the best rate of climb speed.

2. Start looking at the general layout and prominent features.
3. High-level inspection for orientation, approaches, and general suitability.
4. Turn downwind and prepare for low-level inspection. Fuel selection, pump on, mixture rich, pitch fine, carb heat and cowl flaps as required.
5. Descending turn.
6. Note the direction and the reciprocal on your heading indicator.
7. Low-level inspection of the surface.
8. Climbing turn on to the reciprocal.
9. Downwind do landing checks.
10. Tell ATC you will phone them after landing.
11. Descending turn on to finals.
12. Select flap and airspeed for a short-field landing.
13. Touch down, raise flap, and use short-field braking.
14. Stop.
15. Walk over ground before taxiing.

Approach and Landing

Use POH short-field approach and landing technique plus the following guide:

- Use the maximum flap that will permit a safe go-around.
- Approach at the minimum safe speed considering the wind and load.
- Anticipate wind shear.
- The approach should not be a low, flat daisy-cutter.
- Don't approach so high that it is almost a glide.

- Approach fairly steeply, using power to bring you just short of the fence.
- There should be almost no float before touchdown.
- The landing should be at stall speed with the nose high.
- After touchdown, raise the flaps (not the gear!).
- Keep the stick back and brake as firmly as conditions allow.

If any of this is contrary to the POH, do what the POH says.

A precautionary pattern and landing offers plenty of scope to display common sense and airmanship. The pattern must be planned intelligently. Keep your passengers briefed and tell ATC of your intentions.

Remember to phone ATC after landing.

Don't forget carb heat. The conditions that call for a precautionary are often conducive to carb icing.

On finals for the inspection run and for the landing, don't turn in too close or too high. This will cause the speed to increase during the descent. Also remember that flying too close to the cloud base will greatly reduce your visibility.

CROSSWIND TAKEOFF AND LANDING

She may not tell you that she wants a crosswind takeoff or landing. She might simply select a crosswind runway. She expects you to use crosswind techniques if there is a crosswind.

For a crosswind takeoff, use power in the normal way. Do it smoothly and positively, and keep your hand on the throttle.

Anticipate weathercocking and counteract it with positive rudder input to stay straight down the centerline.

Hold the ailerons fully into wind at the start of the takeoff run. As the airspeed increases, use enough aileron to keep the wings level.

Use the elevator to keep the aircraft firmly on the ground, but don't grind the nosewheel into the runway. Make sure that there is no tendency for the aircraft to get light on its wheels and be dragged sideways across the runway.

Lift off positively. You must either be firmly on the ground or firmly in the air — so keep it on the ground 5–10 kts faster than normal, then lift off briskly.

As you lift off, level the ailerons, otherwise you will have one wing down.

The transition between running on the ground and flying must be crisp — but not violent. If you try to ease gently into the air, you will start skidding sideways as the wheels lose their grip.

After liftoff, lower the nose to the level attitude and accelerate to climb speed. Use aileron and rudder for a coordinated turn into wind so that you track along the centerline.

In the Pattern

- Keep a good lookout and listen for traffic using the normal into-wind runway.
- Be sure that ATC knows of your intention to use the crosswind runway.
- Expect crosswind and base legs to be stretched or compressed by the wind.
- Allow for drift on the downwind leg.
- Anticipate and allow for drift in the turns.
- Operate within the POH crosswind limitations.

The Approach and Landing

It's time to get over this nonsense about two types of approach and landing. There is only one sensible way. Do a crabbing approach with the nose slightly into wind and the ball in the middle. Shortly before touchdown, use the rudder to get the nose straight and lower the into-wind wing to counteract drift.

Touch down normally but banked into wind, so you land on one wheel. Straighten the rudder before the nosewheel touches.

Some pilots like to approach faster and flapless. This has little merit — in fact, it has two things against it. First, it involves a lower, flatter approach, which gets you thrown around in ground turbulence. And second, it leaves you very light on your wheels after touchdown. A normal full-flap approach is steeper, which means you spend less time in ground turbulence; it also means that after touchdown you can raise the flaps so the aircraft sits firmly on its wheels. *Tell her you are being careful to raise the flaps and not the gear.*

If you prefer the faster, flapless, sideslipping approach or the kick-straight landing, discuss it with the examiner before the flight.

Either way, she will be looking for control of drift during the approach and landing, as well as airspeed control during the approach.

Anticipate wind shear and increase the drift allowance as airspeed decreases.

She will want to see you touch down on the centerline with the nosewheel straight, and then be positive with directional control and with the ailerons to prevent a wing lifting.

SIDESLIPPING

She is expecting to see:

- You first establish a glide at the correct speed and whatever flap setting she calls for. Remember that some POHs prohibit sideslipping with flap (Cessna 100 and 200 series).
- She will ask you to either maintain a particular heading (keep the nose on a distant point) or maintain a particular track (normally along a runway, but she may select a line feature like a road or a coastline).
- Enter by smoothly applying aileron and sufficient opposite rudder to keep the nose either on the point or to one side of the line feature.
- Increase control input until either the aileron or the rudder reaches the stops. Tell her that this has happened. After that, use the other control to maintain direction.
- Maintain airspeed with the elevator.
- Keep a good lookout for other traffic throughout.
- If she wants a prolonged sideslip (which is unlikely) remember to do engine warm-ups every 1,000'.
- To recover, slowly and smoothly return aileron and rudder to their neutral positions while either keeping the nose on the point or allowing the nose to line up with the line feature.
- During recovery, make sure the airspeed doesn't run away — it's a common fault.
- Remember that the *fuel goes where the ball goes.* So the fuel will move outwards and away from the tank outlet on the lower wing. This 'unporting' can cause the engine to fail particularly if the fuel level is low. So

select the tank on the upper wing before starting. For a left sideslip select the right hand tank, and vice-versa.

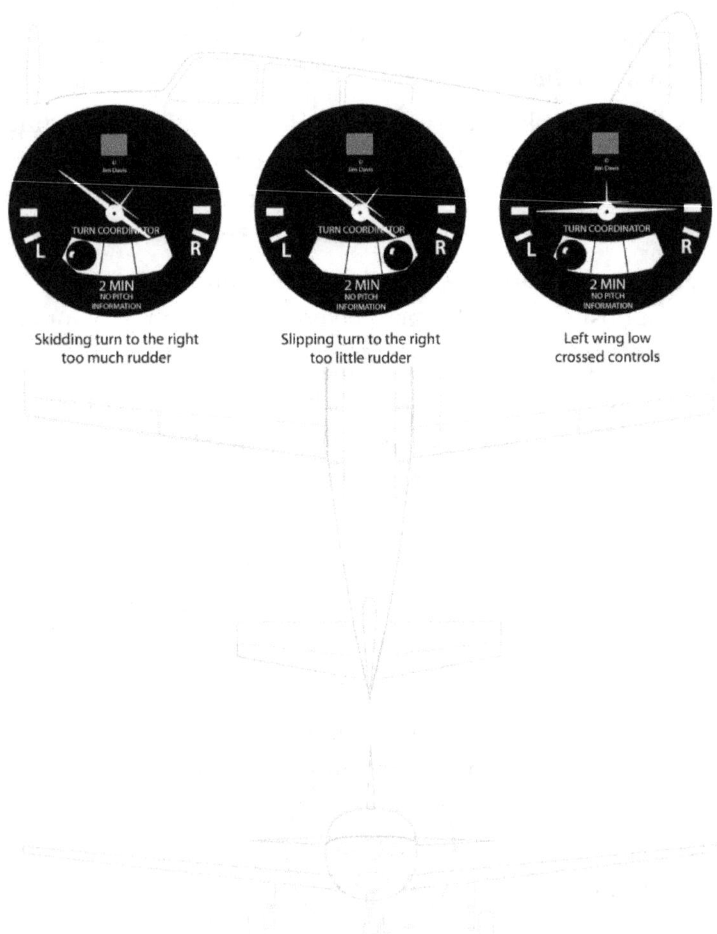

BASIC INSTRUMENT FLYING

When using a full panel under simulated instrument conditions, you must be able to:

- Fly straight and level.
- Do a 180° rate-1 turn in either direction.
- Climb.
- Descend.
- Recognize and recover from the start of a classic graveyard spiral.
- Recognize and recover from unusual attitudes with the nose both high and low.
- Manage emergencies such as vacuum failure.
- Fly one real, or simulated, instrument approach.

NORMAL PATTERN AND LANDING

Here's what she will expect after takeoff:

- Climb at the best rate of climb speed (or a nominated speed).
- Maintain the extended centerline of the runway.
- Do your after-takeoff checks.
- At 500' AGL, lookout and do a climbing turn.
- Check that you are tracking square with the runway.
- Level off at circuit altitude. (Slower aircraft do a climbing turn on to downwind.)
- Lookout and turn parallel with the runway.
- Do your landing checks.
- Make your downwind call opposite the tower.
- Remember to say 'full stop' or 'touch-and-go.'
- Lookout and turn on to base leg. Allow for drift.
- Second flap, airspeed to approach plus 10 kts, reduce power to start descent.
- Lookout, particularly on long finals and opposite base, then turn finals.
- Use the third notch of flap and reduce to your approach speed.
- Allow for drift.
- Call the tower: 'finals touch-and-go' or 'finals full stop.'
- She may want you to do a go-around from a full-flap approach. Use FULL power immediately. Do not let the nose come above the level attitude until you have climb speed. Bleed the flaps off gently. Some aircraft don't like the gear raised immediately — do whatever the POH says.

If she wants you to do a flapless landing, remember not to select flap on downwind when you do your landing checks. Extend the downwind leg to allow for the longer and flatter approach. Remember that your airspeed on base and finals will be about 10 kts faster than normal.

JOINING THE PATTERN

If you are at a controlled airfield, follow ATC instructions. If you are at an uncontrolled field, here's the drill:

At about 10 miles out, call: 'Wilbur traffic, Cherokee ABC approaching from the west, descending through 4,500 ft. We will be joining overhead at 2,000' AGL at 0843.'

At 2,000' AGL, fly to the right of the windsock. Note the windsock, landing T, and other signals.

Call: 'Wilbur traffic, Cherokee ABC overhead at 2,000' AGL, descending for left-hand crosswind on runway 03.'

Turn left to get yourself onto the dead side of the pattern.

Descend to 1,000' AGL and cross the upwind end of the runway at 90°.

Keep a good lookout for traffic in the air or on the ground.

Join a normal downwind leg. Call: 'Wilbur traffic, Cherokee ABC, left downwind for 03.'

Call: 'Wilbur traffic, Cherokee ABC, finals full stop, 03.'

There's a strong tendency at a strange field to make your pattern too close — don't do it.

She will be watching:

- Where you turn base and start descending — it affects your approach.
- Your ability to keep on the centerline, and to counteract drift and turbulence.
- Your overall judgment, smoothness, and coordination.
- Your landing is smooth, nose high, on the centerline, and near the threshold.
- Your use of the rudders to positively maintain direction after touchdown.
- Your general airmanship, lookout, and use of the radio.

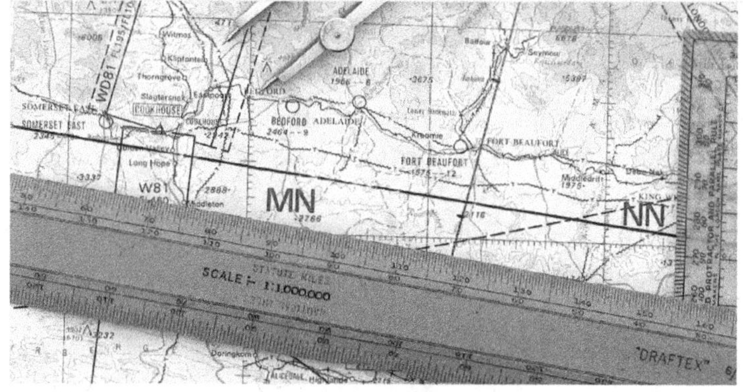

CROSS-COUNTRY FLIGHT

Preparation

She will ask you to file a flight plan with ATC. She is going to check it, so make it neat and correct and you are off to a good start.

Your flight log must contain all the information you are going to need. It should also be neat and legible, even in turbulence or poor light.

It must show your checkpoints, times, distances, speeds, and so on. It should also show the latest weather, and radio and nav-aid frequencies. It must show diversion information — routes, frequencies, weather, and so on. And have a fuel log section.

In your nav-bag you should have:

- A copy of the flight plan.
- Your flight log.
- All the charts for the proposed flight, plus diversions.
- At least two sharp pencils.
- An eraser.
- A scale rule.

- A protractor.
- Your navigation computer (E6-B or equivalent).

Make sure your aircraft is ready for the flight and contains sufficient fuel and oil for the flight plus diversions, plus at least 45 minutes reserve. It must also contain all emergency equipment and documentation applicable to the flight.

Get all this done long before she turns up. There's no hurry and there's no reason why you shouldn't get 100% for preparation.

Fixing Position by Map Reading

Write in the time you set heading — much depends on it!

Keep the chart properly oriented with the track pointing along the fore-and-aft axis of the aircraft.

Do not jump to conclusions when identifying places or landmarks.

Find at least five features that confirm the place is the one you think it is. Use roads, railroads, bridges, rivers, mountains, mines, airfields, and so on for this.

Use common sense. If your groundspeed and time don't tie up, then your identification is suspect.

Map-read all the time – you will always know where you are.

If you can't identify some minor feature, don't despair and don't alter heading — look at the big picture. If in doubt, get up-sun of the place — visibility is far better looking away from the sun.

Fixing Position by Radio Bearing

She will ask you to demonstrate that you can use the VOR. Get to know the equipment on the ground — it makes your life a lot easier in the air.

Identify the station's code before you use it. You must be able to work out an approximate position using the VOR.

Diversion Procedures

At some point — normally on the second or third leg — she will ask you to divert to X. This is a common-sense thing. If there is a pretty direct road or rail line, follow it. If there isn't and she wants an immediate diversion, guess the heading and time. You will be surprised by how accurate it is. Change flight level and notify ATC.

Course Steadiness

You have worked out an accurate heading, so fly it accurately. Don't be tempted to ease to one side because you feel you are slightly off course. Only alter heading when you have positive proof that it is necessary. Then stick solidly to the new heading.

It's much easier to steer on distant features than to chase a heading.

Check the DI against the compass at least once every 10 minutes.

Airspeed and fuel burn are based on POH figures, so set up the power accurately and lean the mixture carefully using POH procedures.

Airspeed and Altitude

Don't try to chase a particular airspeed. If you use the POH power settings you will get close enough to POH cruise speed. The examiner will make allowances for airspeed variations caused by turbulence.

Once you have set up cruise power and leaned the mixture, don't fiddle. Correct altitude changes of up to a couple of hundred feet with the elevator. If they get bigger than that, you may have to richen the mixture, climb properly, set up your power, and lean out again.

You must understand the difference between altitudes and flight levels and use them correctly with the local QNH or standard setting.

Try to keep exactly at your altitude or flight level. A variation of 200' is not good enough. There is no reason to be out by more than 50' in calm air.

You get serious brownie points for keeping an accurate flight log. All you have to do is fill in your ETAs and ATAs and keep a fuel log. Couldn't be easier.

FREDA Checks

Use these checks about every 10 minutes, or whenever you approach an airfield where you will be landing.

Also use them at navigation checkpoints and turning points. (Examples on pages 65 -- 67)

ATC Procedures

We discussed pattern procedures at controlled and uncontrolled fields earlier.

For a cross-country, use the call sign as per the flight plan. Then ATC pulls up your flight plan and knows all about you. Your radio work consists almost entirely of position reports. These are often a weak part so here an example:

Sequence	What you say
Place you are calling	*Kansas City Center*
Who you are	*Cessna 12345*
Where you are (or were)	*Springfield VOR*
The time you were there	*1520*
Your flight level or altitude	*Flight level 080*
Your next reporting point	*Estimating Branson*
Your ETA there	*1535*
Your Destination and ETA	*Joplin 1550*

It is very simple. Do it properly and get her and ATC on your side.

AFTER-FLIGHT PROCEDURES

Engine Stopping Drill

Know your aircraft. Some engines need to run down for the turbocharger. Others like to idle for temperature stabilization. In any case, before shutdown check:

- Engine instruments normal.
- All radios off.
- All unnecessary electrics off.
- Park-brake on.
- Flaps retracted.
- Magneto dead-cut check.
- Cowl flaps set according to the POH.
- Mixture to idle-cutoff.
- Magnetos off.
- Master switch off.

Leaving the Aircraft Checks

- Be sure that the aircraft is parked intelligently.
- Check that all switches are off.
- Engage the control locks.
- Secure the doors and windows.
- Do a post-flight inspection to make sure it is airworthy and undamaged.
- Fit the pitot cover and other covers.
- Use the chocks.
- Tie it down if necessary.

TOLERANCES

Flight test handling tolerances for pilot reviews and licensing (such as the Private or Commercial Pilot License) are standardized to ensure consistent safety and proficiency. While specific numbers can vary slightly by regulatory authority (e.g., FAA, EASA, Transport Canada), the following table represents the standard performance criteria for common flight maneuvers as of April 2026.

Standard Pilot Flight Test Tolerances

Maneuver / Phase of Flight	Altitude Tolerance	Heading / Track Tolerance	Airspeed Tolerance
Straight & Level Flight	±100 feet	±10°	±10 knots
Steep Turns (45° bank)	±100 feet	±10° at rollout	±10 knots
Slow Flight	±100 feet	±10°	+10/ – 5 knots
Stall Recovery	Minimize loss	±10°	Recommended speed
VFR Stabilized Approach	---	±5° of centerline	+10/ – 5 knots
Instrument (IFR) Tracking	±100 feet	< 3/4 scale deflection	±10 knots
Takeoff & Initial Climb	---	±10°	+10/ – 5 knots

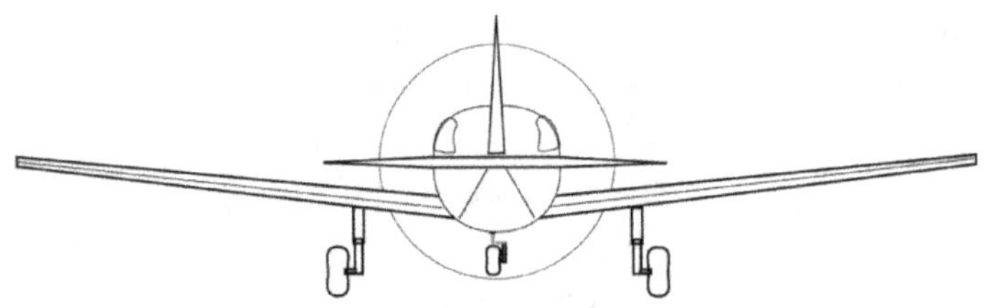

CHECKLISTS – CHECKLISTS – CHECKLISTS

These are a vital part of your flight test - and your life expectancy.

There are no 'standard' or 'correct' checklists but most instructors and flight schools have their own. Whichever ones you use should at least cover what the POH says.

Here's a selection of examples of mnemonic based checklists some of which I found in Air News article by Phil Scott, author of *Then and Now: How Airplanes Got This Way.*

Beware non-specific terms like *Electrics,* or *Instruments.*

ENGINE SHUTDOWN

Mixture, mags, master.

REQUIRED DOCUMENTS

ARROW

A Airworthiness Certificate
R Registration
R Radio station license (not for local flights)
O Operating manual
W Weight and balance

ENGINE FAILURE – SINGLE

GGG

G Glass (instruments)
G Glass
G Grass

GLIDE

G Glide speed
L Landing spot
I Identify problem and remedy it if possible
D Discuss situation Mayday into the radio and
E Emergency (squawk 7700), and Emergency checklist

ENGINE FAILURE – TWIN

MUCK ME

M Maximum power

U Undercarriage Up

C Check which engine has failed – and verify

K Kill it.

M Mags

E Electric

LANDING (Downwind)

GUMP

G Gas

U Undercarriage

M Mixture

P Prop

BUMPFF

B Brakes

U Undercarriage

M Mixture

P Pitch

F Fuel

F Flaps

BEFORE TAKEOFF

*Too **M**any **P**ilots **G**o **F**lying **I**n **H**eaven (**L**ights)*

T Throttle friction, Trim & Transponder set

M Mixture, Mags & Master

P Pitot Cover & heat, Primer, Propeller

G Gyros set

F Flaps, Fuel selectors & quantity check

I Instruments & annunciators ok

H Harnesses and hatches

L Landing lights On

BEFORE CROSS COUNTRY TAKEOFF

CRAFT

C Cleared
R Route
A Altitude
F Frequency
T Transponder

ENGINE FAILURE AFTER TAKEOFF

SFFF

S Speed
F Field
F Fuel
F Flaps

AFTER TAKEOFF (basic)

BFF

B Brakes
F Fuel
F Flaps

AFTER TAKEOFF (complex)

BUPPMFF

B Brakes
U Undercarriage
P Power
P Pitch
M Mixture
F Fuel
F Flaps

ABOUT Jim's Famous Live Cowards Club

If you are in love with flying and airplanes, you've found your home.

Forty years ago, while working as a career flight instructor, I realized something that saved my life: a hell of a lot of aircraft accidents are caused by pilots being too "brave". So I decided to become a **coward**.

I learned to be cowardly about fuel reserves, flying in crap weather, skimping on preflight inspections and having soggy brakes.

I founded the **Live Cowards Club (LCC)** as an informal badge of honor for pilots who are brave enough to say **NO** when it matters.

Being a member has served me well for over 15,000 hours, and it can work for you, too.

Subscribe now. It's FREE! (and you get a certificate.)

http://livecowardsclub.com

www.ingramcontent.com/pod-product-compliance
Lightning Source LLC
LaVergne TN
LVHW010941110826
845149LV00013B/2713

* 9 7 9 8 9 9 5 8 7 8 1 0 0 *